# Whistleblower Protections Under Federal Law: An Overview

**Jon O. Shimabukuro**
Legislative Attorney

**L. Paige Whitaker**
Legislative Attorney

September 13, 2012

Congressional Research Service
7-5700
www.crs.gov
R42727

CRS Report for Congress
*Prepared for Members and Committees of Congress*

# Summary

Legal protections for employees who report illegal misconduct by their employers have increased dramatically since the late 1970s when such protections were first adopted for federal employees in the Civil Service Reform Act of 1978. Since that time, with the enactment of the Whistleblower Protection Act of 1989, Congress has expanded such protections for federal employees. Congress has also established whistleblower protections for individuals in certain private-sector employment through the adoption of whistleblower provisions in at least 18 federal statutes. Among these statutes is the Sarbanes-Oxley Act, the FDA Food Safety Modernization Act, and the Dodd-Frank Wall Street Reform and Consumer Protection Act (Dodd-Frank Act).

In general, claims for relief under the 18 federal statutes follow a similar pattern. Complaints are typically filed with the Secretary of Labor, and an investigation is conducted. Following the investigation, an order is issued by the Secretary, and a party aggrieved by the order is generally permitted to appeal the Secretary's order to a federal court. However, because 18 different statutes are involved in prescribing whistleblower protections, some notable differences exist. For example, under the Department of Defense Authorization Act of 1987, individuals employed by defense contractors who engage in whistleblowing activities file complaints with the Inspector General rather than the Secretary of Labor. Under some of the statutes, including the Commercial Motor Vehicle Safety Act and the Dodd-Frank Act, the Secretary's preliminary order will become a final order if no objections are filed within a prescribed time period.

This report provides an overview of key aspects of the 18 selected federal statutes applicable to individuals in certain private-sector industries. It focuses on the protections provided to employees who believe they have been subject to retaliation, rather than on how or where alleged misconduct should be disclosed. In addition, the report also includes an overview of the Whistleblower Protection Act. While state law may also provide whistleblower protections for employees, this report focuses only on the aforementioned federal statutory provisions.

# Contents

Clean Air Act (CAA) .................................................................................................................... 1
Commercial Motor Vehicle Safety Act (CMVSA) ...................................................................... 2
Comprehensive Environmental Response Compensation and Liability Act of 1980
 (CERCLA) ................................................................................................................................ 3
Department of Defense Authorization Act of 1987 ..................................................................... 4
Dodd-Frank Wall Street Reform and Consumer Protection Act (Dodd-Frank Act) ................... 4
Energy Reorganization Act of 1974 (ERA) ................................................................................. 6
Fair Labor Standards Act of 1938 (FLSA) .................................................................................. 7
FDA Food Safety Modernization Act (FDA Modernization Act) ............................................... 8
Federal Mine Safety and Health Act (FMSHA) .......................................................................... 8
Federal Water Pollution Control Act of 1972 (FWPCA) ............................................................ 9
Longshore and Harbor Workers' Compensation Act (LHWCA) ............................................... 10
Migrant and Seasonal Agricultural Worker Protection Act (MSAWPA) .................................. 10
Occupational Safety and Health Act of 1970 (OSH Act) .......................................................... 11
Safe Drinking Water Act (SDWA) ............................................................................................ 11
Sarbanes-Oxley Act of 2002 (SOX) .......................................................................................... 12
Solid Waste Disposal Act (SWDA) ........................................................................................... 12
Surface Mining Control and Reclamation Act (SMCRA) ......................................................... 13
Toxic Substances Control Act (TSCA) ..................................................................................... 14
Whistleblower Protection Act (WPA) ....................................................................................... 15
    Covered Employees ............................................................................................................ 15
    Protected Disclosures ......................................................................................................... 16
    Personnel Actions ............................................................................................................... 16
    Forums Where Whistleblower Protections May Be Raised ............................................... 17
        Employee Appeals to the MSPB Under Chapter 77 ..................................................... 17
        Actions by the Office of Special Counsel (OSC) ......................................................... 18
        Individual Right of Action (IRA) .................................................................................. 21

# Contacts

Author Contact Information ....................................................................................................... 22

Legal protections for employees who report illegal misconduct by their employers have increased dramatically since the late 1970s when such protections were first adopted for federal employees in the Civil Service Reform Act of 1978. Since that time, with the enactment of the Whistleblower Protection Act of 1989, as amended, Congress has expanded such protections for federal employees. Congress has also established whistleblower protections for individuals in certain private-sector employment through the adoption of whistleblower provisions in at least 18 other industry-specific federal statutes. For example, in 2002, Congress passed the Sarbanes-Oxley Act (SOX) in response to corporate scandals that occurred in the late 1990s and early 2000s. SOX established new civil protections for employees who report concerns about alleged fraud upon shareholders. More recently, Congress passed the FDA Food Safety Modernization Act (FDA Modernization Act), which prohibits entities engaged in food manufacturing, processing, and related activities from discharging or otherwise discriminating against an employee for providing information related to any violation or act that the employee reasonably believes to be a violation of the Federal Food, Drug, and Cosmetic Act.[1]

This report provides an overview of whistleblower provisions in 19 selected federal statutes. While state law may also provide whistleblower protections for employees, this report focuses on relevant federal statutory provisions. The report does not discuss the qui tam and whistleblower provisions of the False Claims Act that permit private citizens with knowledge of fraud against the federal government to sue on its behalf and receive a portion of the recovered proceeds. For discussion of the False Claims Act, see CRS Report R40785, *Qui Tam: The False Claims Act and Related Federal* Statutes, by Charles Doyle.

# Clean Air Act (CAA)

The CAA prohibits an employer from discharging or otherwise discriminating against any employee with respect to his or her compensation, terms, conditions, or privileges of employment because the employee (1) commenced or is about to commence a proceeding under the CAA or a proceeding for the administration or enforcement of any requirement imposed by the CAA; (2) testified or is about to testify in any such proceeding; or (3) assisted or participated or is about to assist or participate in any manner in such a proceeding.[2] Any employee who believes that he or she has been discharged or otherwise discriminated against in violation of the CAA may, within 30 days after such violation occurs, file a complaint with the Secretary of Labor. Upon receipt of the complaint, the Secretary will conduct an investigation and within 30 days of the receipt of such complaint, shall notify the complainant and the alleged violator with the results of the investigation. Within 90 days of receipt of the complaint, the Secretary shall issue an order either providing relief or denying the complaint. If the Secretary determines that a violation has occurred, the Secretary will order the person who committed such violation to (1) take affirmative action to abate the violation, and (2) reinstate the complainant to his or her former position with compensation, including back pay, terms, conditions, and privileges of employment. The Secretary may order the payment of compensatory damages to the complainant. If an order is issued, at the request of the complainant, the Secretary will assess against the person against whom the order is issued a sum equal to the aggregate amount of all costs and expenses,

---

[1] P.L. 111-353, 124 Stat. 3885.
[2] 42 U.S.C. § 7622(a).

including attorneys' and expert witness fees, reasonably incurred by the complainant in bringing the complaint.[3]

Any person adversely affected or aggrieved by an order issued under the CAA's whistleblower provisions may obtain review of the order in the U.S. court of appeals for the circuit in which the violation allegedly occurred. The petition for review must be filed within 60 days from the issuance of the Secretary's order, and the commencement of proceedings shall not, unless ordered by the court, operate as a stay of the Secretary's order. An order by the Secretary is not subject to judicial review in any criminal or other civil proceeding. When a person has failed to comply with an order, the Secretary may file a civil action in the U.S. district court in which the violation occurred and the district courts shall have jurisdiction to grant all appropriate relief, including injunctive relief, as well as compensatory and exemplary damages.[4] Any person on whose behalf an order was issued may commence a civil action against the person to whom such order was issued to require compliance, and the appropriate U.S. district court shall have jurisdiction, without regard to the amount in controversy or citizenship of the parties. In issuing any final order, the court may award costs of litigation, including reasonable attorney and expert witness fees, to any party whenever the court determines it is appropriate.[5]

> The Secretary may file a civil action in the U.S. district court in which the violation occurred when a person has failed to comply with an order.

## Commercial Motor Vehicle Safety Act (CMVSA)

The CMVSA prohibits employers from discharging, disciplining, or discriminating against an employee regarding pay, terms, or privileges of employment because the employee filed a complaint or instituted a proceeding related to a violation of a commercial motor vehicle safety regulation, standard, or order, or has testified or will testify in such proceeding. Additionally, any employee who refuses to operate a vehicle because the operation violates a regulation, standard, or order related to commercial motor vehicle safety or health, or has a reasonable apprehension of serious injury because of the vehicle's unsafe condition, is likewise protected from such retaliatory action.[6]

An employee alleging discharge, discipline, or discrimination in violation of the CMVSA may file a complaint with the Secretary of Labor within 180 days after the alleged violation occurred. Within 60 days of receiving the complaint, the Secretary will conduct an investigation, decide whether the complaint has merit, and notify the complainant and the person alleged to have committed the violation of the findings. If the Secretary determines that it is reasonable to believe that the violation occurred, the Secretary will include in the findings a preliminary order for relief. Within 30 days of receiving notice of the Secretary's findings, the complainant and person alleged to have committed the violation may file objections to the findings or preliminary order and request a hearing on the record, although the filing of objections does not stay a reinstatement ordered in the preliminary order. If a hearing is not requested within 30 days, the preliminary

---

[3] 42 U.S.C. § 7622(b).
[4] 42 U.S.C. § 7622(d).
[5] 42 U.S.C. § 7622(e).
[6] 49 U.S.C. § 31105(a).

order is final and not subject to judicial review. A hearing shall be conducted expeditiously, and not later than 120 days after the end of the hearing, the Secretary will issue a final order. Before the final order is issued, the proceeding may be ended by settlement agreement by the Secretary, the complainant, and the person alleged to have committed the violation. If the Secretary determines that a violation of this provision occurred, he or she can order the person alleged to have committed the violation to (1) take affirmative action to abate the violation; (2) reinstate the complainant to the former position with the same pay and terms and privileges of employment; and (3) pay compensatory damages, including back pay. Upon request by the complainant, the Secretary may assess against the person against whom the order is issued the costs, including attorneys' fees, reasonably incurred by the complainant in bringing the complaint.[7]

Within 60 days after an order is issued, a person adversely affected may file a petition for review in the U.S. court of appeals for the circuit in which the violation occurred or the person resided on the date of the violation. The review will be heard and decided expeditiously and an order is not subject to judicial review in a criminal or other civil proceeding. If a person fails to comply with an order issued under this provision, the Secretary will bring a civil action to enforce the order in the U.S. district court for the judicial district in which the violation occurred.[8]

# Comprehensive Environmental Response Compensation and Liability Act of 1980 (CERCLA)

CERCLA, also known as the "Superfund" Act, prohibits an employer from firing or in any other way discriminating against, or causing to be fired or discriminated against, any employee because that employee provided information to a state or the federal government; filed, instituted, or caused to be filed or instituted any proceeding under the statute; or has testified or will testify in a proceeding resulting from the administration or enforcement of the statute.[9] Any employee who believes that he or she has been terminated or otherwise discriminated against by any person in violation of CERCLA's whistleblower provisions may, within 30 days, apply to the Secretary of Labor for a review of the termination or alleged discrimination. Upon receipt of such application, the Secretary will institute an investigation and upon receiving the investigation report, make findings of fact. If the Secretary finds that a violation occurred, she will issue a decision, incorporating an order, requiring the party committing the violation to take such affirmative action to abate the violation as the Secretary deems appropriate, including reinstatement to the former position with compensation. If she finds no violation, the Secretary will issue an order denying the application. An order issued by the Secretary is subject to judicial review.[10] When an order is issued under this provision, at the request of the applicant, a sum equal to the aggregate amount of all costs and expenses, including attorneys' fees, will be assessed against the person committing such violation.[11]

---

[7] 49 U.S.C. § 31105(b).
[8] 49 U.S.C. § 31105(c), (d).
[9] 42 U.S.C. § 9610(a).
[10] 42 U.S.C. § 9610(b).
[11] 42 U.S.C. § 9610(c).

## Department of Defense Authorization Act of 1987

The Department of Defense Authorization Act of 1987 prohibits defense contractors from discharging, demoting, or otherwise discriminating against an employee as a reprisal for disclosing to a Member of Congress, an authorized official of an agency, or the Department of Justice information relating to a substantial violation of law related to a contract, including the competition for or negotiation of a contract.[12] Any person who believes that he or she has been subject to a prohibited reprisal may submit a complaint to the Inspector General (IG), who is required to investigate the complaint unless the IG determines that the complaint is frivolous. Upon completion of the investigation, the IG will submit a report of the findings of the investigation to the individual, relevant contractor, and the head of the agency.[13] If the agency head determines that a contractor has subjected a person to a prohibited reprisal, the agency head may take one or more of the following actions: (1) order the contractor to abate the reprisal; (2) order the contractor to reinstate the person to the position that the person held before the reprisal, together with compensation, including back pay, employment benefits, and other applicable terms and conditions of employment; (3) order the contractor to pay the complainant an amount equal to the aggregate amount of all costs and expenses, including attorneys' and expert witnesses' fees, that were reasonably incurred by the complainant.[14] If a person fails to comply with such an order, the agency head will file an action for enforcement in the U.S. district court for the district in which the reprisal occurred. The court may grant appropriate relief, including injunctive relief, as well as compensatory and exemplary damages.[15] Within 60 days after the order is issued, any person adversely affected or aggrieved by such an order may obtain review in the U.S. court of appeals for a circuit in which the reprisal occurred.[16]

> Defense contractor employees who engage in whistleblowing activities file complaints with the Inspector General (IG) rather than the Secretary of Labor.

## Dodd-Frank Wall Street Reform and Consumer Protection Act (Dodd-Frank Act)

The Dodd-Frank Act established several new whistleblower protections for individuals employed in the financial services industry. Section 748 of the Dodd-Frank Act, for example, amended the Commodity Exchange Act (CEA) to prohibit employers from discharging or otherwise discriminating against an individual for providing information related to a violation of the CEA to the Commodity Futures Trading Commission (CFTC) or for assisting in any investigation or judicial or administrative action of the CFTC based upon or related to such information. An individual who alleges a termination or other discrimination in violation of the CEA provisions may bring an action in the appropriate district court of the United States. If the individual is a federal employee, he or she must bring the action in accordance with Section 1221 of Title 5, U.S.

---

[12] 10 U.S.C. § 2409(a).
[13] 10 U.S.C. § 2409(b).
[14] 10 U.S.C. § 2409(c)(1).
[15] 10 U.S.C. § 2409(c)(2).
[16] 10 U.S.C. § 2409(c)(3).

Code.[17] An individual who prevails in a whistleblower action will be awarded reinstatement, back pay with interest, and compensation for any special damages sustained as result of the discharge or discrimination, including litigation costs and reasonable attorney's fees.

Section 922 of the Dodd-Frank Act amended the Securities Exchange Act of 1934 to add a new Section 21F that prohibits employers from discharging or otherwise discriminating against an individual for (1) providing information related to a violation of the securities laws to the Securities and Exchange Commission (SEC); (2) initiating, testifying in, or assisting in any investigation or judicial or administrative action of the SEC based upon or related to such information; or (3) making disclosures that are required by SOX, the Securities Exchange Act of 1934, or any other law subject to the SEC's jurisdiction. An individual who alleges a termination or other discrimination in violation of these provisions may bring an action in the appropriate district court of the United States. An individual who prevails in a whistleblower action under Section 21F will be awarded reinstatement, two times the amount of back pay otherwise owed to the individual, with interest, and compensation for litigation costs, expert witness fees, and reasonable expenses.

> An individual who prevails in an action under Section 21F will be awarded two times the amount of back pay otherwise owed.

Section 1057 of the Dodd-Frank Act prohibits employers engaged in providing consumer financial products or services, and employers that provide a material service in connection with the provision of such products or services, from terminating or in any other way discriminating against a covered employee because the employee has (1) provided, caused to be provided, or is about to provide or cause to be provided, information relating to a violation of Title X of the Dodd-Frank Act or any other provision of law that is subject to the jurisdiction of the Bureau of Consumer Financial Protection (Bureau) to the employer, the Bureau, or a state, local, or federal government authority or law enforcement agency; (2) testified or will testify in any proceeding resulting from the administration or enforcement of Title X of the Dodd-Frank Act or any other provision of law that is subject to the jurisdiction of the Bureau; (3) filed, instituted, or caused to be filed or instituted any proceeding under any federal consumer financial law; or (4) objected to or refused to participate in any activity that the employee reasonably believed to be in violation of any law subject to the jurisdiction of, or enforceable by, the Bureau.[18]

An employee who believes that he or she has been discharged or otherwise discriminated against in violation of the Section 1057 whistleblower provisions may file a complaint with the Secretary of Labor within 180 days of the alleged violation. Within 60 days after receiving the complaint, the Secretary will initiate an investigation and determine whether there is reasonable cause to believe that the complaint has merit. The Secretary will notify the complainant and the person alleged to have committed the violation of her determination in writing. If the Secretary concludes that there is reasonable cause to believe that a violation has occurred, she will also issue a preliminary order that provides relief. Either party may file objections to the Secretary's findings or order and request a hearing within 30 days after receiving her notification. If a hearing is not requested in the 30-day period, the preliminary order shall be deemed a final order that is not subject to judicial review.[19]

---

[17] See P.L. 111-203, § 748, 124 Stat. 1376, 1739 (2010).

[18] P.L. 111-203, § 1057(a), 124 Stat. 1376, 2031 (2010). The term "covered employee" is defined to include "any individual performing tasks related to the offering or provision of a consumer financial product or service."

[19] P.L. 111-203, § 1057(c)(2)(C), 124 Stat. 1376, 2032-33 (2010).

If a hearing is conducted, the Secretary is required to issue a final order providing relief or denying the complaint within 120 days after the date of the hearing's conclusion. If the Secretary determines that a violation has occurred, she may order the person who committed the violation to take affirmative action to abate the violation, order the reinstatement of the complainant to his or her former position with compensation, including back pay, and order the payment of compensatory damages. At the request of the complainant, the Secretary will also assess against the person who committed the violation a sum equal to the aggregate amount of all legal costs and expenses reasonably incurred. Any person adversely affected or aggrieved by a final order may seek review of the order in the U.S. court of appeals for the circuit in which the violation allegedly occurred or the circuit in which the complainant resided on the date of such violation. If the Secretary fails to issue a timely final order, the complainant may seek *de novo* review in the appropriate district court of the United States having jurisdiction.

# Energy Reorganization Act of 1974 (ERA)

The ERA prohibits employers from discharging or otherwise discriminating against any employee who (1) notified his or her employer of an alleged violation of the ERA or the Atomic Energy Act of 1954 (AEA); (2) refused to engage in any unlawful practice under the ERA or AEA, if the employee identified the alleged illegality to the employer; (3) testified before Congress or at any federal or state proceeding regarding any provision of the ERA or AEA; (4) commenced a proceeding under the ERA or AEA; (5) testified or is about to testify in any such proceeding; or (6) assisted or participated or is about to assist or participate in a proceeding to carry out the purposes of the ERA or AEA.[20] Any employee who believes that he or she has been discharged or otherwise discriminated against in violation of the ERA's whistleblower provisions may, within 180 days after such violation occurs, file a complaint with the Secretary of Labor alleging such discharge or discrimination. Upon receipt of a complaint, the Secretary will complete an investigation within 30 days. Within 90 days of receiving the complaint, the Secretary will, unless the proceeding is terminated due to a settlement, issue an order either providing relief or denying the complaint. Upon the conclusion of a public hearing and the issuance of a recommended decision that the complaint has merit, the Secretary will issue a preliminary order providing relief, but may not order compensatory damages pending a final order.

If the Secretary determines that a violation has occurred, she will order the person who committed such violation to (1) take affirmative action to abate the violation, and (2) reinstate the complainant to his former position together with compensation, including back pay, terms, conditions, and privileges of his or her employment. The Secretary may order the person who committed the violation to provide compensatory damages to the complainant. If an order is issued, the Secretary, at the request of the complainant, will assess a sum equal to the aggregate amount of all costs and expenses, including attorneys' and expert witness fees, reasonably incurred by the complainant. The Secretary will dismiss a complaint and not conduct an investigation unless the complainant has made a prima facie showing that the protected action by the employee was a contributing factor in the unfavorable personnel action alleged in the complaint.

> The Secretary will dismiss a complaint and not conduct an investigation unless the complainant has made a prima facie showing that the protected action was a contributing factor in the alleged unfavorable personnel action.

Notwithstanding a finding by the Secretary that the complainant has made the required prima

---

[20] 42 U.S.C. § 5851(b).

facie showing, no investigation shall be conducted if the employer demonstrates, by clear and convincing evidence, that it would have taken the same unfavorable personnel action in the absence of such behavior. Relief may not be ordered if the employer demonstrates by clear and convincing evidence that it would have taken the same unfavorable personnel action in the absence of such behavior.[21]

Any person adversely affected by an order issued under the ERA's whistleblower provisions may obtain review of the order in the U.S. court of appeals for the circuit in which the violation allegedly occurred. A petition for review must be filed within 60 days of the issuance of the Secretary's order. Review shall conform to chapter 7 of Title 5, U.S. Code, and the commencement of proceedings under this provision shall not, unless ordered by the court, operate as a stay of the Secretary's order.

An order by the Secretary shall not be subject to judicial review in any criminal or other civil proceeding. Whenever a person fails to comply with an order issued under this provision, the Secretary may file a civil action in the U.S. district court for the district in which the violation occurred. In actions brought under this provision, the district courts shall have jurisdiction to grant all appropriate relief, including injunctive relief and compensatory and exemplary damages. Any person on whose behalf an order was issued may commence a civil action against the person to whom such order was issued to require compliance with such order; the appropriate U.S. district court shall have jurisdiction, without regard to the amount in controversy or citizenship of the parties; and in issuing any final order under this subsection, the court may award costs of litigation, including reasonable attorney and expert witness fees.[22]

# Fair Labor Standards Act of 1938 (FLSA)

The FLSA prohibits employers from discharging or otherwise discriminating against an employee because such employee filed a complaint or instituted any proceeding under the statute, testified or is about to testify in any such proceeding, or served or is about to serve on an industry committee.[23] Employers who willfully violate the FLSA's anti-retaliation provisions may be fined up to $10,000 and imprisoned up to six months. Employers who retaliate against employees in violation of this provision shall be liable for legal and equitable relief, including, without limitation, reinstatement, the payment of lost wages, and an additional equal amount as liquidated damages. An action may be maintained against any employer, including a public agency, in any federal or state court of competent jurisdiction by any one or more employees. The court shall, in addition to any judgment awarded, allow reasonable attorneys' fees to be paid to the plaintiff, as well as the costs of the action. An employee loses his or her right to file a complaint under this provision once the Secretary of Labor files a complaint against the employer.[24]

> Willful violations of the FLSA's anti-retaliation provisions could result in fines up to $10,000 and imprisonment up to six months.

---

[21] Id.
[22] 42 U.S.C. § 5851(c).
[23] 29 U.S.C. § 215(a)(3).
[24] 29 U.S.C. § 216(b).

# FDA Food Safety Modernization Act (FDA Modernization Act)

The FDA Modernization Act amended the Federal Food, Drug, and Cosmetic Act to prohibit an entity engaged in the manufacture, processing, packing, transporting, distribution, reception, holding, or importation of food from discharging or otherwise discriminating against an employee with respect to the individual's compensation, terms, conditions, or privileges of employment because the employee (1) provided, caused to be provided, or is about to provide or cause to be provided information relating to a violation of the Federal Food, Drug, and Cosmetic Act to the employer, the federal government, or the attorney general of a state; (2) testified or is about to testify in a proceeding concerning the violation; (3) assisted or participated or is about to assist or participate in a proceeding concerning the violation; or (4) objected to, or refused to participate in any activity that the employee believed to be in violation of the Federal Food, Drug, and Cosmetic Act.[25]

An individual who believes that he or she has been discharged or otherwise discriminated against in violation of the relevant whistleblower provisions may file a complaint with the Secretary of Labor within 180 days after the date on which the violation occurs.[26] Within 60 days of receiving the complaint, the Secretary will initiate an investigation and determine whether there is reasonable cause to believe that the complaint has merit. If the Secretary determines that reasonable cause exists, she will accompany her findings with a preliminary order that requires the person who committed the violation to take affirmative action to abate the violation, to reinstate the complainant to his or her former position with compensation, and to provide compensatory damages. The person alleged to have committed the violation or the complainant may file objections to the findings or the preliminary order and request a hearing. A final order must be issued by the Secretary within 120 days after the date of the hearing's conclusion. If the Secretary fails to issue a timely final decision, the complainant may seek *de novo* review in the appropriate district court of the United States with jurisdiction

# Federal Mine Safety and Health Act (FMSHA)

The FMSHA prohibits an employer from discharging an employee or applicant for employment because the individual (1) filed or made a complaint under or related to the FMSHA; (2) is the subject of medical evaluations and potential transfer; (3) instituted or testified in any proceeding under or related to the FMSHA; or (4) exercised any statutory right afforded by the FMSHA.[27] Employees and applicants who believe that they have been discharged, interfered with, or otherwise discriminated against in violation of this prohibition may file a complaint with the Secretary of Labor within 60 days after the alleged violation. Upon receipt of the complaint, the Secretary will forward a copy to the respondent and within 15 days of receiving the complaint, the Secretary will institute an investigation as she deems appropriate. If the Secretary determines that the complaint was not brought frivolously, the Federal Mine Safety and Health Review Commission will order the immediate reinstatement of the miner pending a final order. If the

---

[25] 21 U.S.C. § 1012(a).
[26] 21 U.S.C. § 1012(b)(1).
[27] 30 U.S.C. § 815(c)(1).

Secretary determines that the FMSHA's whistleblower provisions have been violated, she will immediately file a complaint with the Commission, with service upon the alleged violator and miner, proposing an order granting appropriate relief. The Commission shall afford an opportunity for a hearing and shall issue an order,

> If the Secretary determines that the complaint was not brought frivolously, the Federal Mine Safety and Health Review Commission will order the immediate reinstatement of the miner pending final order.

affirming, modifying, or vacating the Secretary's proposed order, or directing other appropriate relief. The Commission retains the authority to require a person committing a violation to abate the violation as the Commission deems appropriate, including the rehiring or reinstatement of the miner to his or her former position with back pay and interest.[28]

Within 90 days of receiving a complaint, the Secretary will notify the miner about whether a violation occurred. If the Secretary determines that the FMSHA's whistleblower provisions were violated, the complainant shall have the right to file an action in his or her own behalf before the Commission. The Commission shall afford an opportunity for a hearing and shall issue an order, granting such relief as it deems appropriate. Whenever an order is issued sustaining a complainant's charges, a sum equal to the aggregate amount of all costs and expenses, including attorneys' fees, will be assessed against the person who committed the violation. Any person adversely affected by such an order may obtain review in any U.S. court of appeals for the circuit in which the violation is alleged to have occurred or in the U.S. Court of Appeals for the D.C. Circuit.[29]

# Federal Water Pollution Control Act of 1972 (FWPCA)

The FWPCA prohibits an employer from firing or otherwise discriminating against an employee, or causing such firing or discrimination, because the employee has filed, instituted, or caused to be filed or instituted any proceeding under the FWPCA, or has testified or is about to testify in any proceeding resulting from the administration or enforcement of the FWPCA.[30] Any employee who believes that he or she has been fired or discriminated against in violation of this provision may, within 30 days after such alleged violation occurs, apply to the Secretary of Labor for a review. Upon receipt of such application, the Secretary will institute an investigation as he or she deems appropriate. Upon receiving the report of such investigation, the Secretary will make findings of fact; if she finds that such violation did occur, the Secretary will issue a decision, incorporating an order and findings, requiring the party committing such violation to take such affirmative action to abate the violation, including the rehiring or reinstatement of the employee with compensation. If the Secretary finds that there was no such violation, she will issue an order denying the application; such order shall be subject to judicial review in the same manner as orders and decisions are subject to judicial review under 33 U.S.C. §§ 1251 *et seq.* Whenever an order is issued, at the request of the applicant, a sum equal to the aggregate amount of all costs and expenses, including attorneys' fees, determined to have been reasonably incurred by the applicant, will be assessed against the person committing the violation.

---

[28] 30 U.S.C. § 815(c)(2).
[29] 30 U.S.C. § 816.
[30] 33 U.S.C. § 1367(a).

# Longshore and Harbor Workers' Compensation Act (LHWCA)

The LHWCA prohibits an employer from discharging or otherwise discriminating against an employee who claims or attempts to claim compensation from the employer, or testifies or is about to testify against the employer in a proceeding under the statute. Any employer who violates this provision will be liable for a penalty of not less than $1,000 nor more than $5,000. If such penalties are not paid, they may be recovered in a civil action brought in the appropriate U.S. district court. Any employee that is discriminated against under the statute's whistleblower provisions shall be restored to his or her employment and shall be compensated for any loss of wages arising from the discrimination, provided that if the employee ceases to be qualified to perform the duties of employment, he or she shall not be entitled to such restoration and compensation. The employer and not his insurance carrier shall be liable for such penalties and payments, and any provision in an insurance policy undertaking to relieve the employer from the liability for such penalties and payments shall be void.[31]

> If the employee ceases to be qualified to perform the duties of employment, the employee will not be restored to his or her position and will not be compensated for any wage loss.

# Migrant and Seasonal Agricultural Worker Protection Act (MSAWPA)

The MSAWPA prohibits employers from intimidating, threatening, restraining, coercing, blacklisting, discharging, or in any manner discriminating against any migrant or seasonal agricultural worker because such worker has, with just cause, filed a complaint or instituted, or caused to be instituted, any proceeding under the statute's anti-retaliation provisions. Additionally, any employee who has testified or is about to testify in any such proceeding or justifiably exercises any right or protection afforded by MSAWPA is protected from retaliatory action.[32] An employee who believes, with just cause, that he or she has been discriminated against in violation of the relevant provisions may file a complaint with the Secretary of Labor within 180 days of the violation. As she deems appropriate, the Secretary will institute an investigation and, upon determining that a violation has occurred, will bring an action in any appropriate U.S. district court. In any such action, the U.S. district court will have jurisdiction, for cause shown, to restrain the violation and order all appropriate relief, including reinstatement with back pay or damages.[33]

---

[31] 33 U.S.C. § 948a.
[32] 29 U.S.C. § 1855(a).
[33] 29 U.S.C. § 1855(b).

# Occupational Safety and Health Act of 1970 (OSH Act)

The OSH Act prohibits employers from discharging or in any manner discriminating against an employee because such employee filed a complaint or instituted or caused to be instituted a proceeding under the OSH Act, or is about to testify in any such proceeding. Additionally, any employee who has testified or is about to testify in any such proceeding or exercises any right or protection afforded by the OSH Act is protected from retaliatory action. An employee who believes that he or she has been discharged or otherwise discriminated against in violation of the OSH Act may file a complaint with the Secretary of Labor alleging such discrimination within 30 days. Upon receipt of such complaint, the Secretary will institute an investigation as she deems appropriate. If the Secretary determines that a violation has occurred, she will bring an action in any appropriate U.S. district court. The U.S. district court shall have jurisdiction, for cause shown, to restrain the violation and order all appropriate relief including reinstatement with back pay.[34]

# Safe Drinking Water Act (SDWA)

The SDWA prohibits employers from firing, or in any other way discriminating against, or causing to be fired or discriminated against, any employee because such employee filed, instituted, or caused to be filed or instituted any proceeding under the SDWA or has testified or is about to testify in any proceeding resulting from the administration or enforcement of the SDWA. Any employee who believes that he or she has been fired or otherwise discriminated against in violation of the SDWA may, within 30 days after such alleged violation occurs, apply to the Secretary of Labor for a review. Upon receipt of such application, the Secretary will initiate an investigation as she deems appropriate. Upon receiving the report of such investigation, the Secretary will make findings of fact; if she finds that such violation did occur, the Secretary will issue a decision, incorporating an order and findings, requiring the party committing such violation to take such affirmative action to abate the violation, including, the rehiring or reinstatement of the employee with compensation. If the Secretary finds that there was no such violation, she will issue an order denying the application; such order is subject to judicial review in the same manner as orders and decisions are subject to judicial review under 42 U.S.C. §§ 6901 *et seq.* Whenever an order is issued, at the request of the applicant, a sum equal to the aggregate amount of all costs and expenses, including attorneys' fees, determined to have been reasonably incurred by the applicant, shall be assessed against the person who committed the violation.[35]

Any employee or employer adversely affected or aggrieved by an order may obtain review of the order in the U.S. court of appeals for the circuit in which the violation allegedly occurred. Within 60 days of the issuance of the order, the petition for review must be filed and review shall conform to 5 U.S.C. §§ 701 *et seq.* An order of the Secretary shall not be subject to judicial review in any criminal or other civil proceeding. Whenever a person has failed to comply with an order, the Secretary will file a civil action in the U.S. district court for the district in which the violation

---

[34] 29 U.S.C. § 660(c).
[35] 42 U.S.C. § 300j-9(i)(1),(2).

occurred. In actions brought under the SDWA's whistleblower provisions, the district courts shall have jurisdiction to grant all appropriate relief, including injunctive relief and compensatory and exemplary damages.[36]

## Sarbanes-Oxley Act of 2002 (SOX)

SOX prohibits publicly traded companies, including any subsidiaries or affiliates whose financial information is included in the consolidated financial statements of such companies, and nationally recognized statistical rating organizations from discharging, demoting, suspending, threatening, harassing, or in any other manner discriminating against an employee because such employee provided information, caused information to be provided, otherwise assisted in an investigation or filed, testified, or participated in a proceeding regarding any conduct that the employee reasonably believes is a violation of SOX, any SEC rule or regulation, or any federal statute relating to fraud against shareholders, when the information or assistance is provided to a federal regulatory or law enforcement agency, any Member or committee of Congress, or a person with supervisory authority over the employee or investigative authority for the employer, regarding any violation of 18 U.S.C. §§ 1341 (mail fraud), 1343 (wire fraud), 1344 ( bank fraud), 1348 (securities fraud against shareholders), or any SEC rule or regulation, or of any federal law regarding fraud against shareholders.[37] Any employee who alleges such wrongful discharge or other discrimination may file a complaint with the Secretary of Labor, using procedures set forth in 49 U.S.C. § 42121(b). In the absence of delay resulting from an employee's bad faith, the employee may seek *de novo* review in the appropriate U.S. district court, if the Secretary of Labor does not issue a final decision within 180 days. An action must be commenced within 180 days after the date on which the violation occurs.[38]

A prevailing employee may be awarded all relief necessary to make the individual whole, including reinstatement with pre-discrimination seniority status, back pay with interest, and compensation for any special damages incurred as a result of the discrimination, including litigation costs, expert witness fees, and reasonable attorneys fees, and to leave the employee with all rights, privileges or remedies under federal or state law or any collective bargaining agreement.[39]

> An employee prevailing in a whistleblower action may be awarded all relief necessary to make the individual whole.

## Solid Waste Disposal Act (SWDA)

The SWDA prohibits employers from firing, or in any other way discriminating against, or causing to be fired or discriminated against, any employee because such employee filed, instituted, or caused to be filed or instituted any proceeding under the SWDA, or has testified or is about to testify in any proceeding resulting from the administration or enforcement of the

---

[36] 42 U.S.C. § 300j-9(i)(3),(4).

[37] 18 U.S.C. § 1514A(a).

[38] 18 U.S.C. § 1514A(b)(2)(D).

[39] 18 U.S.C. § 1514A(c), (d).

SWDA.[40] Any employee who believes that he or she has been fired or otherwise discriminated against in violation of the SWDA's whistleblower provisions may, within 30 days after such alleged violation occurs, apply to the Secretary of Labor for a review. Upon receipt of such application, the Secretary will institute an investigation as she deems appropriate. Following the receipt of the investigation report, the Secretary will make findings of fact; if she finds that a violation did occur, the Secretary will issue a decision, incorporating an order and findings, requiring the party committing such violation to take such affirmative action to abate the violation, including the rehiring or reinstatement of the employee with compensation. If the Secretary finds no violation, she will issue an order denying the application; such order shall be subject to judicial review in the same manner as orders and decisions are subject to judicial review under 42 U.S.C. §§ 6901 *et seq*.[41] Whenever an order is issued, at the request of the applicant, a sum equal to the aggregate amount of all costs and expenses, including attorneys' fees, to have been reasonably incurred by the applicant, will be assessed against the person who committed the violation.[42]

# Surface Mining Control and Reclamation Act (SMCRA)

The SMCRA prohibits employers from discharging or in any other way discriminating against or causing to be fired or discriminated against any employee because such employee has filed, instituted, or caused to be filed or instituted any proceeding under this provision. Additionally, any employee who has testified or is about to testify in any such proceedings is protected from such retaliatory action.[43] An employee who believes that he or she has been fired or otherwise discriminated against in violation of the SMCRA's whistleblower provisions may, within 30 days, apply to the Secretary of Labor for a review of such firing or alleged discrimination. Upon receipt of such complaint, the Secretary will initiate an investigation as she deems appropriate. If the Secretary determines that a violation occurred, she will issue a decision incorporating the findings of fact and an order requiring the party committing the violation to take such affirmative action to abate the violation as the Secretary deems appropriate, including the rehiring or reinstatement of the employee with compensation. If the Secretary finds that no violation occurred, she shall issue a finding. Orders issued by the Secretary shall be subject to judicial review in the same manner as other orders and decisions of the Secretary are subject to judicial review under the SMCRA.[44] Whenever an order is issued to abate a violation, at the request of the applicant, a sum equal to the aggregate amount of all costs and expenses, including attorney's fees, determined to have been reasonably incurred by the applicant in connection with the institution and prosecution of such proceedings, shall be assessed against the person who committed the violation.[45]

---

[40] 42 U.S.C. § 6971(a).
[41] 42 U.S.C. § 6971(b).
[42] 42 U.S.C. § 6971(c).
[43] 30 U.S.C. § 1293(a).
[44] 30 U.S.C. § 1293(b).
[45] 30 U.S.C. §1293(c).

# Toxic Substances Control Act (TSCA)

The TSCA prohibits employers from discharging or otherwise discriminating against any employee with respect to compensation, terms, conditions, or privileges of employment because the employee has (1) commenced, caused to be commenced, or is about to commence or cause to be commenced a proceeding under the TSCA; (2) testified or is about to testify in any such proceeding; or (3) assisted or participated or is about to assist or participate in such a proceeding or in any other action to carry out the purposes of the TSCA.[46] Any employee who believes that he or she has been discharged or otherwise discriminated against by any person in violation of the TSCA's whistleblower provisions may, within 30 days after such alleged violation occurs, file a complaint with the Secretary of Labor. Upon receipt of such a complaint, the Secretary will conduct an investigation and within 30 days of the receipt of such complaint, the Secretary will complete such investigation. Within 90 days of receiving the complaint, the Secretary will, unless the proceeding is terminated due to a settlement, issue an order either providing relief or denying the complaint. The Secretary may not enter into a settlement terminating a proceeding on a complaint without the participation and consent of the complainant. If the Secretary determines that a violation of this provision has occurred, the Secretary will (1) order the person who committed such violation to take affirmative action to abate the violation, (2) order such person to reinstate the complainant to the complainant's former position together with the compensation, including backpay, terms, conditions, and privileges of the complainant's employment, (3) order compensatory damages, and (4) where appropriate, order exemplary damages. Whenever an order is issued, at the request of the applicant, a sum equal to the aggregate amount of all costs and expenses, including attorneys' fees will be assessed against the person who committed the violation.[47] Any employee or employer adversely affected or aggrieved by an order may obtain review of the order in the U.S. court of appeals for the circuit in which the violation allegedly occurred. The petition for review must be filed within 60 days of the issuance of the order. Such review must conform to 5 U.S.C.§§ 701 *et seq*. Whenever a person has failed to comply with an order, the Secretary will file a civil action in the U.S. district court for the district in which the violation was found to occur. In actions brought under the TSCA's whistleblower provisions, the district courts shall have jurisdiction to grant all appropriate relief, including injunctive relief and compensatory and exemplary damages.[48]

---

[46] 15 U.S.C. § 2622(a).
[47] 15 U.S.C. § 2622(b).
[48] 15 U.S.C. § 2622(c),(d).

# Whistleblower Protection Act (WPA)

The WPA[49] generally provides protections for federal employees who make disclosures evidencing illegal or improper government activities. In order to trigger the protections of the WPA, a case must contain the following elements: a "personnel action" that was taken because of a "protected disclosure" made by a "covered employee."

> To trigger protections under the WPA, a case must contain the following elements, as defined under the act:
> - A personnel action
> - A protected disclosure
> - A covered employee

## Covered Employees

Although anyone may disclose whistleblowing information for referral to the appropriate agency, an investigation and report from the head of that agency is required only if the information is received from a "covered employee." In addition, with few exceptions, prohibited personnel practices apply only to covered employees. Therefore, as a threshold matter, it is important to note which federal employees are statutorily covered.

Generally, current employees, former employees, or applicants for employment to positions in the executive branch of government and the Government Printing Office, in both the competitive and the excepted service, as well as positions in the Senior Executive Service, are considered covered employees.[50] However, those positions that are excepted from the competitive service because of their "confidential, policy-determining, policy-making, or policy-advocating character,"[51] and any positions exempted by the President based on a determination that it is necessary and warranted by conditions of good administration,[52] are not protected by the whistleblower statute.

Moreover, the statute does not apply to federal workers employed by the U.S. Postal Service or the Postal Rate Commission,[53] the Government Accountability Office, the Federal Bureau of Investigation,[54] the Central Intelligence Agency, the Defense Intelligence Agency, the National Geospatial-Intelligence Agency, the National Security Agency, and any other executive entity that the President determines primarily conducts foreign intelligence or counter-intelligence activities.[55] Agency heads are required to inform their employees of these protections.[56]

---

[49] P.L. 101-12, 103 Stat. 16; P.L. 103-424, 108 Stat. 4361 (codified, as amended, in various sections of Title 5 U.S.C.).

[50] 5 U.S.C. § 2302(a)(2)(B).

[51] 5 U.S.C. § 2302(a)(2)(B)(i).

[52] 5 U.S.C. § 2302(a)(2)(B)(ii).

[53] 5 U.S.C. § 2105(e).

[54] Another provision of federal law prohibits personnel practices in the FBI as a reprisal for a disclosure of information to the Attorney General or his or her designee that the employee reasonably believes evidences "(1) a violation of any law, rule, or regulation, or (2) mismanagement, a gross waste of funds, an abuse of authority, or a substantial and specific danger to public health or safety." 5 U.S.C. § 2303(a)(1),(2).

[55] 5 U.S.C. § 2302(a)(2)(C).

[56] 5 U.S.C. § 2302(c).

## Protected Disclosures

Any disclosure of information that a covered employee reasonably believes evidences "a violation of any law, rule, or regulation" or evidences "gross mismanagement, a gross waste of funds, an abuse of authority, or a substantial and specific danger to public health or safety" is protected on the condition that the disclosure is not prohibited by law nor required to be kept secret by Executive Order in the interest of national defense or foreign affairs.[57] Moreover, any disclosure made to the Special Counsel or to the Inspector General of an agency or another employee designated by the head of the agency to receive such disclosures, which the employee reasonably believes evidences "a violation of any law, rule, or regulation," or evidences "gross mismanagement, a gross waste of funds, an abuse of authority, or a substantial and specific danger to public health or safety" is also protected.[58] In addition, the WPA expressly provides that the statute is not to be interpreted as "authoriz[ing] the withholding of information from the Congress or the taking of any personnel action against an employee who discloses information to the Congress."[59]

## Personnel Actions

The WPA protects employees from reprisals in the form of an agency taking or failing to take a "personnel action." This encompasses a broad range of actions by an agency having a negative or adverse impact on the employee. The statute specifically defines the term "personnel action" to include 11 areas of agency activity:

> (i) an appointment; (ii) a promotion; (iii) an action under chapter 75 of this title or other disciplinary or corrective action; (iv) a detail, transfer, or reassignment; (v) a reinstatement; (vi) a restoration; (vii) a reemployment; (viii) a performance evaluation under chapter 43 of this title; (ix) a decision concerning pay, benefits, or awards, or concerning education or training if the education or training may reasonably be expected to lead to an appointment, promotion, performance evaluation, or other action described in this subparagraph; (x) a decision to order psychiatric testing or examination; and (xi) any other significant change in duties, responsibilities, or working conditions.[60]

---

[57] 5 U.S.C. § 2302(b)(8)(A).

[58] 5 U.S.C. § 2302(b)(8)(B).

[59] 5 U.S.C. § 2302(b). Based on the legislative history regarding this provision of the WPA, it appears that Congress sought to protect its right to receive even "confidential" information from federal employees, without employee fear of reprisals:

> The provision is intended to make clear that by placing limitations on the kinds of information any employee may publicly disclose without suffering reprisal, there is not intent to limit the information an employee may provide to Congress or to authorize reprisal against an employee for providing information to Congress. For example, 18 U.S.C. 1905 prohibits public disclosure of information involving trade secrets. That statute does not apply to transmittal of such information by an agency to Congress. Section 2302(b)(8) of this act would not protect an employee against reprisal for public disclosure of such statutorily protected information, but it is not to be inferred that an employee is similarly un-protected if such disclosure is made to the appropriate unit of the Congress. Neither title I nor any other provision of the act should be construed as limiting in any way the rights of employees to communicate with or testify before Congress. H.Rept. 95-1717 (Conference Report) (1978), *reprinted in* 1978 U.S. CODE CONG. & ADMIN. NEWS 2861.

See also 5 U.S.C. § 7211, providing that an employee is guaranteed the right to freely petition or furnish information to Congress, a Member of Congress, a committee, or a Member thereof.

[60] 5 U.S.C. § 2302(a)(2)(A).

The WPA also expressly protects employees from prohibited personnel practices taken because they engaged in activities that are often related to whistleblowing, including exercising any appeal, complaint, or grievance right granted by law, rule, or regulation, testifying for others or lawfully assisting others in any such appeal, complaint, or grievance right; cooperating with or disclosing information to an agency Inspector General or the Special Counsel; or for refusing to obey an order that would be in violation of law.[61]

## Forums Where Whistleblower Protections May Be Raised

Under the WPA, there are three general forums or proceedings where whistleblower protections may be raised: (A) in employee appeals to the Merit Systems Protection Board (MSPB) of an agency's adverse action against the employee under chapter 77;[62] (B) in actions instituted by the Office of Special Counsel (OSC);[63] and (C) in individual rights of action.[64] Beyond the statutory provisions of the WPA, the defense or claim of reprisal for whistleblowing might also be raised in a grievance proceeding initiated by an employee pursuant to a grievance procedure that was negotiated through collective bargaining between the employee's agency and the employee union.[65] An aggrieved employee affected by a prohibited personnel action is precluded from choosing more than one of the above remedies.[66]

> Under the WPA, whistleblower protections may be raised in three general forums or proceedings:
>
> (1) Employee appeals to the MSPB under chapter 77
>
> (2) Actions instituted by the Office of Special Counsel
>
> (3) Individual rights of action

### Employee Appeals to the MSPB Under Chapter 77

The MSPB is authorized to hear and rule on appeals by employees regarding agency actions affecting the employee and that are appealable to the Board by law, rule, or regulation.[67] Types of agency actions against employees that are appealable to the MSPB and in which an employee may raise the defense of reprisal for whistleblowing as a prohibited personnel practice include adverse actions against the employee for "such cause as will promote the efficiency of the service" (generally referred to as conduct-based adverse actions),[68] and performance-based adverse actions against employees for "unacceptable performance."[69] In such appeals, an agency's decision and action will not be upheld if the employee "shows that the decision was based on any prohibited personnel practice described in section 2302(b) of this title."[70] If the MSPB finds that an employee or applicant for employment has prevailed in an appeal, the

---

[61] 5 U.S.C. § 2302(b)(9).
[62] 5 U.S.C. § 7701.
[63] 5 U.S.C. §§ 1211-1215.
[64] 5 U.S.C. § 1221.
[65] 5 U.S.C. § 7121.
[66] 5 U.S.C. § 7121(g)(2).
[67] 5 U.S.C. § 7701, 5 U.S.C. § 1205.
[68] 5 U.S.C. § 7513(a).
[69] 5 U.S.C. § 4303(a).
[70] 5 U.S.C. § 7701(c)(2)(B).

employee or applicant may be provided with interim relief, pending the outcome of any petition of review.[71] Moreover, the Special Counsel may not intervene in an appeal under chapter 77 without the consent of the individual bringing the appeal.[72]

## Actions by the Office of Special Counsel (OSC)

The WPA established the OSC as an agency independent from the MSPB.[73] Its primary responsibilities, however, have remained essentially the same as set forth in its statutory predecessor, the Civil Service Reform Act (CSRA). With the goal of protecting employees, former employees, and applicants for employment from prohibited personnel practices, the OSC has the duty to receive allegations of prohibited personnel practices and to investigate such allegations,[74] as well as to conduct an investigation of possible prohibited personnel practices on its own initiative, absent any allegation.[75]

The Special Counsel has several avenues available through which to pursue allegations, complaints, and evidences of reprisals for whistleblowing activities, including (1) requiring agency investigations and agency reports concerning actions the agency is planning to take to rectify those matters referred;[76] (2) seeking an order for "corrective action" by the agency before the MSPB;[77] (3) seeking "disciplinary action" against officers and employees who have committed prohibited personnel practices;[78] (4) intervening in any proceedings before the MSPB, except that in cases where an individual has brought an individual right of action (IRA) under Section 1221 or an appeal to the MSPB under chapter 77, the OSC must first obtain the individual's consent;[79] and (5) seeking a stay from the MSPB for any personnel action pending an investigation.[80]

### *Investigations*[81]

Within 240 days of receipt of a complaint, the OSC must make a determination as to whether there are reasonable grounds to believe that a prohibited personnel practice has occurred, exists,

---

[71] 5 U.S.C. § 7701(b)(2)(A).

[72] 5 U.S.C. § 1212(c)(2).

[73] 5 U.S.C. § 1211(a). It provides that the Office of Special Counsel (OSC) will be headed by the Special Counsel and have a judicially noted official seal. The Senate report states that although the MSPB and the OSC had "separated themselves administratively in 1984," the whistleblower legislation "completes this process by establishing the OSC as an independent agency." S.Rept. 100-413 at 18. Moreover, the statute provides that the Special Counsel, appointed by the President, with the advice and consent of the Senate, may only be removed from office for "inefficiency, neglect of duty, or malfeasance in office." 5 U.S.C. § 1211(b).

[74] 5 U.S.C. § 1212(a)(2).

[75] 5 U.S.C. § 1214(a)(5).

[76] 5 U.S.C. § 1213(c).

[77] 5 U.S.C. § 1214(b)(2).

[78] 5 U.S.C. § 1215(b).

[79] 5 U.S.C. § 1212(c).

[80] 5 U.S.C. § 1212(b)(1).

[81] In addition to investigating whether prohibited personnel actions have been taken because of protected whistleblowing disclosures, the WPA also charges the OSC with investigating whether there is a "substantial likelihood" that whistleblowing disclosures evidence violations of a law, rule or regulation. 5 U.S.C. §1213(b).

or is to be taken.[82] If a positive determination is made and the information was sent to the Special Counsel by an employee, former employee, applicant for employment, or an employee who obtained the information acting within the scope of employment,[83] the Special Counsel must transmit the information to the appropriate agency head and require that the agency head conduct an investigation and submit a written report.[84] The identity of the complaining employee may not be disclosed without such individual's consent, unless the Special Counsel determines that disclosure is necessary to avoid imminent danger to health and safety or an imminent criminal violation.[85] The Special Counsel then reviews the reports as to their completeness and the reasonableness of the findings[86] and submits the reports to Congress, the President, the Comptroller General,[87] and the complainant.[88]

If the Special Counsel does not make a positive determination, however, he or she may only transmit the information to the agency head with the consent of the individual.[89] Further, if the Special Counsel receives the information from some source other than the ones described above, he or she *may* transmit the information to the appropriate agency head who shall inform the Special Counsel of any action taken.[90] In any case where the subject of the whistleblowing disclosure evidences a criminal violation, however, all information is referred to the Attorney General and no report is transmitted to the complainant.[91]

At least every 60 days throughout its investigation, the OSC must give notice of the status of the investigation to the individual who brought the allegation.[92] In addition, no later than 10 days before the termination of an investigation, a written status report including the proposed findings and legal conclusions must be made to the individual who made the allegation of wrongdoing.[93]

### Corrective Actions

If in any investigation the Special Counsel determines that there are "reasonable grounds to believe" a prohibited personnel practice exists or has occurred, the Special Counsel must report findings and recommendations, and may include recommendations for corrective action, to the MSPB, the agency involved, the Office of Personnel Management (OPM) and, optionally, to the President.[94] If the agency does not act to correct the prohibited personnel practice, the Special Counsel may petition the MSPB for corrective action.[95] The MSPB, before rendering its decision, is required to provide an opportunity for oral or written comments by the Special Counsel, the

---

[82] 5 U.S.C. § 1214(b)(2)(A)(i).
[83] 5 U.S.C. § 1213(c)(2).
[84] 5 U.S.C. § 1213(c)(1).
[85] 5 U.S.C. § 1213(h).
[86] 5 U.S.C. § 1213(e)(2).
[87] 5 U.S.C. § 1213(e)(3).
[88] 5 U.S.C. § 1213(e)(1).
[89] 5 U.S.C. § 1213(g)(2).
[90] 5 U.S.C. § 1213(g)(1).
[91] 5 U.S.C. § 1213(f).
[92] 5 U.S.C. § 1214(a)(1)(C)(ii).
[93] 5 U.S.C. § 1214(a)(1)(D).
[94] 5 U.S.C. § 1214(b)(2)(B).
[95] 5 U.S.C. § 1214(b)(2)(C).

agency involved and the OPM, and for written comments by any individual who alleges to be the victim of the prohibited personnel practices.[96]

The WPA made it easier for a complainant to prove retaliation for whistleblowing in a corrective action before the MSPB. The Special Counsel need only prove by a preponderance of the evidence that the disclosure was a "contributing factor" in the personnel action, instead of a "significant factor."[97] In addition, once the MSPB renders a final order or decision of corrective action, complainants have the right to judicial review in the U.S. Court of Appeals for the Federal Circuit.[98]

In what is probably the most significant change from its statutory predecessor, the CSRA, the WPA increased the standard by which an agency must prove its affirmative defense that it would have taken the personnel action even if the employee had not engaged in protected conduct. Once the complainant's *prima facie* case of reprisal has been established by showing that the whistleblowing was a contributing factor in the personnel action, the government is required to demonstrate by "clear and convincing evidence" that it would have taken the same personnel action even in the absence of such disclosure.[99] Under the CSRA, the government's standard of proof was a "preponderance of the evidence." "Clear and convincing evidence," although a lesser standard than the criminal standard of "beyond a reasonable doubt," is greater than "preponderance of the evidence."

## *Disciplinary Actions*

Proceedings for disciplinary action against an officer or employee who commits a prohibited personnel practice may be instituted by the Special Counsel by filing a written complaint with the MSPB.[100] After proceedings before the MSPB or an administrative law judge,[101] if violations are found, the MSPB may impose any of various disciplinary actions, including removal, reduction in grade, debarment from federal employment for a period not to exceed five years, suspension, reprimand, or an assessment of civil fines up to $1,000.[102] In addition, the agency involved may be held responsible for reasonable attorney's fees.[103] In the case of presidentially appointed and Senate confirmed employees in "confidential, policy-making, policy-determining, or policy-advocating" positions, the complaint and the statement of facts, along with any response from the employee, are to be presented to the President for disposition in lieu of the presentation to the Board.[104]

---

[96] 5 U.S.C. § 1214(b)(3).
[97] 5 U.S.C. §1214(b)(4)(i).
[98] 5 U.S.C. § 1214(c).
[99] 5 U.S.C. § 1214(b)(4)(B).
[100] 5 U.S.C. § 1215(a)(1).
[101] 5 U.S.C. § 1215(a)(2)(C).
[102] 5 U.S.C. § 1215(a)(3).
[103] 5 U.S.C. § 1204(m)(1).
[104] 5 U.S.C. § 1215(b).

## Intervention

As a matter of right, the Special Counsel may intervene or otherwise participate in any proceedings before the MSPB, except that in cases where an individual has brought an individual right of action (IRA) under Section 1221, discussed below, or an appeal to the MSPB under chapter 77, the OSC must first obtain the individual's consent.[105]

## Stays

Upon application by the OSC, a member of the MSPB may stay or postpone, for 45 days, pending an investigation, a personnel action that the Special Counsel has reasonable grounds to believe constitutes a prohibited personnel practice, unless the member determines that a stay would not be appropriate under the circumstances.[106] If no MSPB member acts within three days of the OSC application, the stay becomes effective.[107] After the employing agency has had an opportunity to comment on the appropriateness of extending a stay, the MSPB may extend it.[108] A stay may be terminated by the MSPB at any time, except that a stay may not be terminated by the MSPB on its own motion or on the motion of an agency, unless notice and opportunity for oral or written comments are first provided to the Special Counsel and the individual on whose behalf the stay was ordered; or on a motion of the Special Counsel, unless notice and opportunity for oral or written comments are first provided to the individual on whose behalf the stay was ordered.[109]

# Individual Right of Action (IRA)

The WPA provides that an employee, former employee, or applicant for employment has the independent right to seek review of whistleblower reprisal cases by the MSPB no more than 60 days after notification is provided to such employee that the investigation was closed or 120 days after filing a complaint with the OSC.[110] As a result of the IRA statutory provisions, a greater number of employees, including probationers, temporaries, and those in the excepted service, have a method of appeal to the MSPB for whistleblower reprisals that was not previously available under the CSRA.[111] In addition, retired employees are not barred from instituting this type of appeal.[112]

If the employee is the prevailing party before the MSPB, based on the finding of a prohibited personnel practice, or if the employee is the prevailing party in an appeal to the MSPB, regardless of the basis of the decision, the WPA provides several remedies. These may include placing the individual, as nearly as possible, in the position the individual would have been in had the prohibited personnel practice not occurred, awarding back pay and related benefits, recompensing medical costs incurred, travel expenses, or any other reasonable and foreseeable consequential

---

[105] 5 U.S.C. § 1212(c).
[106] 5 U.S.C. § 1214(b)(1)(A)(i),(ii).
[107] 5 U.S.C. § 1214(b)(1)(A)(iii).
[108] 5 U.S.C. § 1214(b)(1)(B),(C).
[109] 5 U.S.C. § 1214(b)(1)(D).
[110] 5 U.S.C. §§ 1221, 1214(a)(3).
[111] 5 U.S.C. § 7701.
[112] 5 U.S.C. § 1221(j).

charges.[113] In all cases, corrective action includes awarding attorneys' fees.[114] The MSPB findings can be based on circumstantial evidence.[115] Moreover, the Special Counsel may not intervene in an individual right of action without the consent of the individual bringing the appeal.[116]

## Author Contact Information

Jon O. Shimabukuro
Legislative Attorney
jshimabukuro@crs.loc.gov, 7-7990

L. Paige Whitaker
Legislative Attorney
lwhitaker@crs.loc.gov, 7-5477

---

[113] 5 U.S.C. § 1221(g)(1)(A)(i),(ii).
[114] 5 U.S.C. § 1221(g)(1)(B).
[115] 5 U.S.C. § 1221(e)(1).
[116] 5 U.S.C. § 1212(c)(2).

www.ingramcontent.com/pod-product-compliance
Lightning Source LLC
Chambersburg PA
CBHW081247180526
45171CB00005B/571